PENGUIN BOOKS

THE A-Z OF
KNOCK-KNOCK
JOKES

Other collections by
Phillip Adams and Patrice Newell

The Penguin Book of Australian Jokes
The Penguin Book of More Australian Jokes
The Penguin Bumper Book of Australian Jokes
The Penguin Book of Jokes from Cyberspace
The Penguin Book of Schoolyard Jokes
The Penguin Book of All-New Australian Jokes
Pocket Jokes
More Pocket Jokes
What a Joke!
What a Giggle!
What a Laugh!
What a Hoot!

THE A-Z OF
KNOCK-KNOCK
JOKES

COLLECTED BY
Phillip Adams & Patrice Newell

PENGUIN BOOKS

Penguin Books

Published by the Penguin Group (Australia)
250 Camberwell Road, Camberwell, Victoria 3124, Australia
Penguin Books Ltd
80 Strand, London WC2R 0RL, England
Penguin Group (USA) Inc.
375 Hudson Street, New York, New York 10014, USA
Penguin Books, a division of Pearson Canada
10 Alcorn Avenue, Toronto, Ontario, Canada M4V 3B2
Penguin Books (NZ) Ltd
Cnr Rosedale and Airborne Roads, Albany, Auckland, New Zealand
Penguin Books (South Africa) (Pty) Ltd
24 Sturdee Avenue, Rosebank, Johannesburg 2196, South Africa
Penguin Books India (P) Ltd
11, Community Centre, Panchsheel Park, New Delhi 110 017, India

First published by Penguin Books Australia, a division of Pearson
Australia Group, 2003

1 3 5 7 9 10 8 6 4 2

Text and cover design by Miriam Rosenbloom © Penguin Group
(Australia)
Typeset in 11.5/16pt ITC Veljovic by Post Pre-press Group, Brisbane
Printed in Australia by McPherson's Printing Group,
Maryborough, Victoria

National Library of Australia
Cataloguing-in-Publication data:

The A-Z of knock-knock jokes.

ISBN 0 14 300212 0.

1. Knock-knock jokes. 2. Wit and humor. I. Adams, Phillip, 1939–.
II. Newell, Patrice, 1956–.

808.882

www.penguin.com.au

FOREWORD

Knowing it would be knice if you knew more knock-knock jokes, we knocked together this collection of knye-on all the knock-knock jokes on earth. We think you'll find them amusing.

Knock-knock jokes have been around since Kneanderthal times when people knocked on the doors of each other's caves. The Knormans introduced them to England and Martin Luther famously nailed some to the front door of a church. During the Black Death, corpse collectors knocked on front doors, calling upon people to 'bring out their dead', and would break the ice with a knice knock-knock joke or two. And even today, from Knorway to Knew

FOREWORD

England via Knigeria and Knagasaki, the knock-knock joke is used to make knew friends.

We come upon a knock-knock joke by William Shakespeare in *Macbeth*, Act II Scene III, written in 1606: 'Here is a knocking indeed. Knock knock knock. Who's there? I' the name of Beelzebub . . .'. And again, from Lady Macbeth: 'Whence is that knocking? How is't with me when every noise appals me?'

Some scholars argue that the original of Hamlet's soliloquy was 'Knock-knock, who's there?' Only to be replaced during rehearsal with the now familiar enquiry, 'To be or not to be, That is the question.'

Another knock-knock joke was discovered by Howard Carter. It was inscribed with hieroglyphs on the doors of Tutankhamen's tomb. 'Knock-knock, who's there? If thou knows what's good for you, don't enter this tomb. Lest you suffer the curse of the pharoah.'

Simply by memorising the few thousand knock-knock jokes in this book, you'll be prepared for every social circumstance. Knuns tell knock-

FOREWORD

knock jokes to knovices and a majority of judges try one or two before passing the death sentence. If you're kneeling to propose marriage, start with a knock-knock joke. If you're about to sack an employee or ask for a raise, a 'Knock-knock, who's there' is guaranteed to help.

Your editors knoticed an alarming shortage of local knock-knock jokes – so this book includes a few collected in the knever-knever and on the Knullarbor. If you know any others, please drop us a knote.

Whilst the frisbee and the hula hoop come and go, and the yoyo has its ups and downs, the knock-knock joke is forever.

Knock-knock.

Who's there?

1-4.

1-4 who?

1-4 the ladies!

Knock-knock.

Who's there?

1-8.

1-8 who?

1-8 lunch already. Is dinner ready?

Knock-knock.

Who's there?

Aardvark.

Aardvark who?

Aardvark a million miles for one
of your smiles!

Knock-knock.

Who's there?

Aaron.

Aaron who?

Aaron on the side of caution!

Knock-knock.

Who's there?

Abbott.

Abbott who?

Abbott time you answered the door!

Knock-knock.

Who's there?

Abe.

Abe who?

Abe C D E F G H . . .

Knock-knock.

Who's there?

Abyssinia.

Abyssinia who?

Abyssinia behind bars one of these days!

Knock-knock.

Who's there?

Accordion.

Accordion who?

Accordion to the weather forecast
it's gonna snow tomorrow!

Knock-knock.

Who's there?

Ach.

Ach who?

Bless you!

Knock-knock.

Who's there?

Acid.

Acid who?

Acid sit down and be quiet!

Knock-knock.

Who's there?

Ada.

Ada who?

Ada burger for lunch!

Knock-knock.

Who's there?

Adair.

Adair who?

Adair once but I'm bald now!

Knock-knock.

Who's there?

Ahmed.

Ahmed who?

Ahmedeus Mozart!

Knock-knock.

Who's there?

Aida.

Aida who?

Aida lot of sweets and now
I've got a tummy ache!

Knock-knock.

Who's there?

Al.

Al who?

Al give you a kiss if you open this door!

Knock-knock.

Who's there?

Aladdin.

Aladdin who?

Aladdin the street wants a word with you!

Knock-knock.

Who's there?

Alaska.

Alaska who?

Alaska my friend the question then!

Knock-knock.

Who's there?

Alba.

Alba who?

Alba in the kitchen if you need me!

Knock-knock.

Who's there?

Alfalfa.

Alfalfa who?

Alfalfa you, if you give me a kiss!

Knock-knock.

Who's there?

Alfie.

Alfie who?

Alfie terrible if you leave!

Knock-knock.

Who's there?

Alfred.

Alfred who?

Alfred the needle if you sew!

Knock-knock.

Who's there?

Alison.

Alison who?

Alison to you, then you listen to me!

Knock-knock.

Who's there?

Allied.

Allied who?

Allied, so sue me!

Knock-knock.

Who's there?

Alma.

Alma who?

Alma-ny knock-knock jokes can you take?

Knock-knock.

Who's there?

Amana.

Amana who?

Amana bad mood!

Knock-knock.

Who's there?

Ammonia.

Ammonia who?

Ammonia bird in a gilded cage . . .

Knock-knock.

Who's there?

Amory.

Amory who?

Amory Christmas and a Happy New Year!

THE A-Z OF KNOCK-KNOCK JOKES

Knock-knock.

Who's there?

Amos.

Amos who?

A mosquito just bit me!

Knock-knock.

Who's there?

Amy.

Amy who?

Amy 'fraid I've forgotten!

Knock-knock.

Who's there?

Andy.

Andy who?

And he told me another silly knock-knock joke!

Knock-knock.

Who's there?

Avery

Avery who.

Avery merry Christmas!

B

Knock-knock.

Who's there?

Balanchine.

Balanchine who?

Balanchine act!

Knock-knock.

Who's there?

Banana.

Banana who?

Banana split, so ice-creamed!

Knock-knock.

Who's there?

Barbara.

Barbara who?

Barbara black sheep, have you any wool?

Knock-knock.

Who's there?

Banana.

Banana who?

Knock-knock.

Who's there?

Banana.

Banana who?

Knock-knock.

Who's there?

Banana.

Banana who?

Knock-knock.

Who's there?

Orange.

Orange who?

Orange you glad I didn't say banana again?

Knock-knock.

Who's there?

Barber.

Barber who?

Barberd wire!

Knock-knock.

Who's there?

Bargain.

Bargain who?

Bargain up the wrong tree!

Knock-knock.

Who's there?

Bark.

Bark who?

Bark your car on the drive!

Knock-knock.

Who's there?

Baron.

Baron who?

Baron mind who you're talking to!

Knock-knock.

Who's there?

Barrister.

Barrister who?

Barristercratic!

Knock-knock.

Who's there?

Barry.

Barry who?

Barry nice to see you, my friend!

Knock-knock.

Who's there?

Bat.

Bat who?

Bat you'll never guess!

Knock-knock.

Who's there?

Bea.

Bea who?

Beacause I'm worth it!

Knock-knock.

Who's there?

Bean.

Bean who?

Bean working very hard today!

Knock-knock.

Who's there?

Beck.

Beck who?

Beckfast of champions!

Knock-knock.

Who's there?

Becker.

Becker who?

Becker the devil you know!

Knock-knock.

Who's there?

Bed.

Bed who?

Bed you can't guess who I am!

Knock-knock.

Who's there?

Bee.

Bee who?

Bee careful!

Knock-knock.

Who's there?

Beef.

Beef who?

Beef fair now!

Knock-knock.

Who's there?

Beets.

Beets who?

Beets me!

THE A-Z OF KNOCK-KNOCK JOKES

Knock-knock.

Who's there?

Beezer.

Beezer who?

Beezer black and yellow and make honey!

Knock-knock.

Who's there?

Beggar.

Beggar who?

Beggar you won't know!

Knock-knock.

Who's there?

Beirut.

Beirut who?

Beirut force!

Knock-knock.

Who's there?

Berlin.

Berlin who?

Berlin the water to make a cup of tea!

Knock-knock.

Who's there?

Bernie.

Bernie who?

Bernie bridges!

Knock-knock.

Who's there?

Bert.

Bert who?

Bert the dinner!

Knock-knock.
Who's there?
Bertha.
Bertha who?
Bertha-day greetings!

Knock-knock.
Who's there?
Beryl.
Beryl who?
Beryl of beer!

Knock-knock.
Who's there?
Bet.
Bet who?
Bet you don't know who's knocking
on your door!

Knock-knock.

Who's there?

Bette-lou.

Bette-lou who?

Bette-lou a few kilos!

Knock-knock.

Who's there?

Bettina.

Bettina who?

Bettina minute you'll open this door!

Knock-knock.

Who's there?

Betty.

Betty who?

Betty buy Birds Eye!

Knock-knock.

Who's there?

Bhuto.

Bhuto who?

Bhuton the other foot!

Knock-knock.

Who's there?

Biafra.

Biafra who?

Biafraid, be very afraid!

Knock-knock.

Who's there?

Bigotry.

Bigotry who?

Bigotry than the one in your garden!

Knock-knock.

Who's there?

Bingo.

Bingo who?

Bingo-ing to come and see you for ages!

Knock-knock.

Who's there?

Blair.

Blair who?

Blair of Greeks bearing gifts!

Knock-knock.

Who's there?

Blue.

Blue who?

Blue away with the wind!

Knock-knock.

Who's there?

Blue.

Blue who?

Blue your nose!

Knock-knock.

Who's there?

Blur.

Blur who?

Blur, it's cold and wet out here!

Knock-knock.

Who's there?

Bobby.

Bobby who?

Bobbyn up and down like this!

Knock-knock.

Who's there?

Boiler.

Boiler who?

Boiler egg for four minutes!

Knock-knock.

Who's there?

Bolivia.

Bolivia who?

Bolivia me, I know what I'm talking about!

Knock-Knock-knock.

Who's there?

Bolton.

Bolton who?

Bolton the door!

Knock-knock.

Who's there?

Boo.

Boo who?

Don't cry, it's only a joke!

Knock-knock.

Who's there?

Bowl.

Bowl who?

Bowl me over!

Knock-knock.

Who's there?

Brad.

Brad who?

Brad news, I'm afraid!

Knock-knock.

Who's there?

Bradman.

Bradman who?

Bradman and Robin!

Knock-knock.

Who's there?

Brazil.

Brazil who?

Brazil support a girl's chest!

Knock-knock.

Who's there?

Brendan.

Brendan who?

Brendan ear to what I have to say . . .

Knock-knock.

Who's there?

Brother.

Brother who?

Brother-ation, I've forgotten your name!

Knock-knock.

Who's there?

Bruce.

Bruce who?

I Bruce easily, don't hit me!

Knock-knock.

Who's there?

Bruno.

Bruno who?

Bruno more tea for me!

Knock-knock.

Who's there?

Bud.

Bud who?

Bud, Sweat and Tears!

Knock-knock.

Who's there?

Buddha.

Buddha who?

Buddha this slice of bread for me!

Knock-knock.

Who's there?

Buddy.

Buddy who?

Buddy-fingers!

Knock-knock.

Who's there?

Buffer.

Buffer who?

Buffer you can say Jack Robinson!

Knock-knock.

Who's there?

Bug.

Bug who?

Bug Rogers!

Knock-knock.

Who's there?

Bug.

Bug who?

Bug-sy Malone!

Knock-knock.
Who's there?
Burglar.
Burglar who?
Burglars don't knock!

Knock-knock.
Who's there?
Burns.
Burns who?
Burns me up!

Knock-knock.
Who's there?
Burton.
Burton who?
Burton the hand is worth two in the bush!

Knock-knock.

Who's there?

Bush.

Bush who?

Bush your money where your mouth is!

Knock-knock.

Who's there?

Buster.

Buster who?

Buster blood vessel!

Knock-knock.

Who's there?

Butcher.

Butcher who?

Butcher left leg in, put your left leg out . . .

Knock-knock.

Who's there?

Butter.

Butter who?

Butter wrap up, it's cold out here!

Knock-knock.

Who's there?

Button.

Button who?

Button in is not polite!

Knock-knock.

Who's there?

Byron.

Byron who?

Byron new suit!

Knock-knock.

Who's there?

C's.

C's who?

C's the day!

Knock-knock.

Who's there?

Candy.

Candy who?

Candy you go any faster?

Knock-knock.

Who's there?

Cantaloupe.

Cantaloupe who?

Cantaloupe with you tonight!

Knock-knock.

Who's there?

Canto.

Canto who?

Canto your change!

Knock-knock.

Who's there?

Card.

Card who?

Card you see it's me?

Knock-knock.

Who's there?

Cargo.

Cargo who?

Cargo better if you fill it with petrol first!

Knock-knock.

Who's there?

Carl.

Carl who?

Carl get you there quicker than if you walk!

Knock-knock.

Who's there?

Carlene.

Carlene who?

Carlene against that wall?

Knock-knock.

Who's there?

Carlo.

Carlo who?

Carlo-ad of junk!

Knock-knock.

Who's there?

Carlotta.

Carlotta who?

Carlotta trouble when it breaks down!

Knock-knock.

Who's there?

Carmen.

Carmen who?

Carmen get it!

Knock-knock.

Who's there?

Carol.

Carol who?

Carol go if you turn the ignition key!

Knock-knock.

Who's there?

Caroline.

Caroline who?

Caroline of rope with you!

Knock-knock.

Who's there?

Carrie.

Carrie who?

Carrie me home, I'm tired!

Knock-knock.

Who's there?

Carrie.

Carrie who?

Carrie a torch!

Knock-knock.

Who's there?

Carrie.

Carrie who?

Carrie on camping!

Knock-knock.

Who's there?

Carrot.

Carrot who?

Carrot me back home!

Knock-knock.

Who's there?

Carson.

Carson who?

Carcinogenic!

Knock-knock.

Who's there?

Cash.

Cash who?

No, I prefer peanuts!

Knock-knock.

Who's there?

Cash.

Cash who?

Cash me if you can!

Knock-knock.

Who's there?

Cass.

Cass who?

Cass more flies with honey than vinegar!

Knock-knock.

Who's there?

Cassette.

Cassette who?

Cassette your dinner, I'm sorry!

Knock-knock.

Who's there?

Cassie.

Cassie who?

Cassie the forest for the trees!

Knock-knock.

Who's there?

Castor.

Castor who?

Castorblanca!

Knock-knock.

Who's there?

Castro.

Castro who?

Castro bread upon the waters!

Knock-knock.

Who's there?

Cat.

Cat who?

Cat you just open this door?

Knock-knock.

Who's there?

Caterpillar!

Caterpillar who?

Caterpillar a few mice for you!

Knock-knock.

Who's there?

Cathy.

Cathy who?

Cathy the doorbell, it's too dark out here!

Knock-knock.

Who's there?

Catskills.

Catskills who?

Catskills mice!

Knock-knock.

Who's there?

Cattle.

Cattle who?

Cattle always purr when you stroke her!

Knock-knock.

Who's there?

Cheese.

Cheese who?

Cheese a jolly good fellow!

Knock-knock.

Who's there?

Cher.

Cher who?

Cher and share alike!

Knock-knock.

Who's there?

Cherry.

Cherry who?

Cherry oh, see you later!

Knock-knock.
Who's there?
Chest.
Chest who?
Chest-nuts for sale!

Knock-knock.
Who's there?
Chester.
Chester who?
Chester minute, don't you recognise me?

Knock-knock.
Who's there?
Chester.
Chester who?
Chester drawers!

Knock-knock.

Who's there?

Chesterfield!

Chesterfield who?

Chesterfield full of cows, nothing else!

Knock-knock.

Who's there?

Chesterfield.

Chesterfield who?

Chesterfield my leg so I gave him a slap!

Knock-knock.

Who's there?

Chicken.

Chicken who?

Chicken your pockets –
I think your keys are there . . .

Knock-knock.
Who's there?
Chile.
Chile who?
Chile out tonight!

Knock-knock.
Who's there?
Chin.
Chin who?
Chin up, I'm not going to tell you any more
knock-knocks!

Knock-knock.
Who's there?
China.
China who?
China just like old times, isn't it!

Knock-knock.

Who's there?

China.

China who?

China late, isn't it?

Knock-knock.

Who's there?

Chloe.

Chloe who?

Chloe's Encounters of the Third Kind!

Knock-knock.

Who's there?

Choc-ice.

Choc-ice who?

Choc-ice into this glass, would you please?

Knock-knock.
Who's there?
Chocs.
Chocs who?
Chocs away!

Knock-knock.
Who's there?
Chopin.
Chopin who?
Chopin list!

Knock-knock.
Who's there?
Chow Mein.
Chow Mein who?
Chow Mein to meet you, my dear!

Knock-knock.

Who's there?

Chrome.

Chrome who?

Chrome-osome!

Knock-knock.

Who's there?

Chuck.

Chuck who?

Chuck and see if the door is locked!

Knock-knock.

Who's there?

Chuck.

Chuck who?

Chuck in a sandwich for lunch!

Knock-knock.

Who's there?

Churchill.

Churchill who?

Churchill be the best place for a wedding!

Knock-knock.

Who's there?

Cicero.

Cicero who?

Cicero the boat ashore!

Knock-knock.

Who's there?

Cigarette.

Cigarette who?

Cigarette life if you don't weaken!

Knock-knock.

Who's there?

Claudette.

Claudette who?

Claudette a whole cake!

Knock-knock.

Who's there?

Claus.

Claus who?

Claus the door, it's freezing in here!

Knock-knock.

Who's there?

Clay.

Clay who?

Clay on, Sam!

Knock-knock.
Who's there?
Clay.
Clay who?
Clay pigeon!

Knock-knock.
Who's there?
Cliff.
Cliff who?
Cliffhanger!

Knock-knock.
Who's there?
Cliff.
Cliff who?
Cliff the hedges!

Knock-knock.
Who's there?
Clinton.
Clinton who?
Clinton your eye!

Knock-knock.
Who's there?
Clive.
Clive who?
Clive every mountain, ford every stream!

Knock-knock.
Who's there?
Closure.
Closure who?
Closure mouth when you're eating!

Knock-knock.

Who's there?

Clown.

Clown who?

Clown for the count!

Knock-knock.

Who's there?

Cockadoodle.

Cockadoodle who?

No, you idiot, it's Cockadoodle doo!

Knock-knock.

Who's there?

Cockatoo.

Cockatoo who?

Cockatoo, cockathree, cockafour . . .

Knock-knock.
Who's there?
Cod.
Cod who?
Cod red-handed!

Knock-knock.
Who's there?
Coda.
Coda who?
Coda paint!

Knock-knock.
Who's there?
Coffin.
Coffin who?
Coffin and spluttering!

Knock-knock.

Who's there?

Cohen.

Cohen who?

Cohen your own way!

Knock-knock.

Who's there?

Cole.

Cole who?

Cole-umbian coffee, the richest coffee
in the world!

Knock-knock.

Who's there?

Colin.

Colin who?

Colin all cars, Colin all cars!

Knock-knock.

Who's there?

Colleen.

Colleen who?

Colleen up your room, it's filthy!

Knock-knock.

Who's there?

Colleen.

Colleen who?

Colleen a spade a spade!

Knock-knock.

Who's there?

Collie.

Collie who?

Collie Miss Molly, I don't know!

Knock-knock.
Who's there?
Collier.
Collier who?
Collier big brother, see if I care!

Knock-knock.
Who's there?
Cologne.
Cologne who?
Cologne me names won't help!

Knock-knock.
Who's there?
Cologne.
Cologne who?
Cologne Ranger is here!

Knock-knock.

Who's there?

Conga.

Conga who?

Conga on meeting like this!

Knock-knock.

Who's there?

Constance Norah.

Constance Norah who?

Constance Norahs make it difficult to sleep!

Knock-knock.

Who's there?

Consumption.

Consumption who?

Consumption be done about all
these knock-knock jokes?

Knock-knock.

Who's there?

Conyers.

Conyers who?

Conyers please open the door?

Knock-knock.

Who's there?

Cook.

Cook who?

Cuckoo yourself, I didn't come
here to be insulted!

Knock-knock.

Who's there?

Cookie.

Cookie who?

Cookie-n the kitchen, it's easier!

Knock-knock.
Who's there?
Coolidge.
Coolidge who?
Coolidge a cucumber!

Knock-knock.
Who's there?
Cosi.
Cosi who?
Cosi has to!

Knock-knock.
Who's there?
Cosmo.
Cosmo who?
Cosmo trouble than you're worth!

Knock-knock.

Who's there?

Costas.

Costas who?

Costas a fortune to get here!

Knock-knock.

Who's there?

Cosy.

Cosy who?

Cosy who's knocking!

Knock-knock.

Who's there?

Cotton.

Cotton who?

Cotton a trap!

Knock-knock.

Who's there?

Courtney.

Courtney who?

Courtney criminals lately?

Knock-knock.

Who's there?

Cousin.

Cousin who?

Cousin stead of opening the door
you've left me out on the doorstep!

Knock-knock.

Who's there?

Cowgo.

Cowgo who?

No silly, cow go moo!

Knock-knock.

Who's there?

Cream.

Cream who?

Cream any louder and the police will come!

Knock-knock.

Who's there?

Crete.

Crete who?

Crete to see you again!

Knock-knock.

Who's there?

Cricket.

Cricket who?

Cricket neck means I can't lift anything!

Knock-knock.

Who's there?

Crispin.

Crispin who?

Crispin crunchy is how I like my apples!

Knock-knock.

Who's there?

Crock.

Crocodile?

No, crock of shit!

Knock-knock.

Who's there?

Crock and Dial.

Crock and Dial who?

Crock and Dial Dundee!

Knock-knock.

Who's there?

Cronkite.

Cronkite who?

Cronkite evidence!

Knock-knock.

Who's there?

Curly.

Curly who?

Curly Q!

Knock-knock.

Who's there?

Curry.

Curry who?

Curry me back home, will you?

Knock-knock.

Who's there?

Cyril.

Cyril who?

Cyril pleasure to meet you again!

Knock-knock.

Who's there?

Czech.

Czech who?

Czech before you open the door!

Knock-knock.
Who's there?
Daniel.
Daniel who?
Daniel so loud!

Knock-knock.
Who's there?
Deesa.
Deesa who?
Deesa-ppear and don't come back!

Knock-knock.
Who's there?
Despair.
Despair who?
Despair tyre is flat!

THE A-Z OF KNOCK-KNOCK JOKES

Knock-knock.

Who's there?

Dexter.

Dexter who?

Dexter halls with boughs of holly!

Knock-knock.

Who's there?

Didgeridoo.

Didgeridoo who?

Didgeridoo what the teacher told you?

Knock-knock.

Who's there?

Diesel.

Diesel who?

Diesel teach me to go knocking on doors!

Knock-knock.

Who's there?

Dime.

Dime who?

Dime to stop telling these knock-knock jokes!

Knock-knock.

Who's there?

Dingo.

Dingo who?

Dingo the toilet, so I'm busting for a pee!

Knock-knock.

Who's there?

Disguise.

Disguise who?

Disguise the limit!

Knock-knock.

Who's there?

Dishes.

Dishes who?

Dishes the stupidest knock-knock joke ever!

Knock-knock.

Who's there?

Dishwasher.

Dishwasher who?

Dishwasher way I talked before
I got my new teeth!

Knock-knock.

Who's there?

Doctor.

Doctor who?

You just said it!

Knock-knock.

Who's there?

Donate.

Donate who?

Doan ate the peas and Doan's brother
ate the carrots!

Knock-knock.

Who's there?

Donut.

Donut who?

Donut open til Christmas!

Knock-knock.

Who's there?

Doris.

Doris who?

Doris locked, I'm a comin' in
through yer window!

Knock-knock.

Who's there?

Dot.

Dot who?

Dot's for me to know and you to find out!

Knock-knock.

Who's there?

Duck.

Duck who?

Duck-uckoo fell out of da clock!

Knock-knock.

Who's there?

Dwayne.

Dwayne who?

Dwayne the tub, I'm dwowning!

Knock-knock.

Who's there?

Eames.

Eames who?

Eames to please!

Knock-knock.

Who's there?

Eamon.

Eamon who?

Eamon in a good mood today, come in!

Knock-knock.

Who's there?

Ear.

Ear who?

Ear you are, I've been looking for you!

THE A-Z OF KNOCK-KNOCK JOKES

Knock-knock.
Who's there?
Earl.
Earl who?
Earl be glad to get to bed, I'm tired!

Knock-knock.
Who's there?
Ears.
Ears who?
Ears some more knock-knock jokes for you!

Knock-knock.
Who's there?
Earwig.
Earwig who?
Earwigo, Earwigo, Earwigo!

Knock-knock.

Who's there?

E. C.

E. C. who?

E. C. Street!

Knock-knock.

Who's there?

Echidna.

Echidna who?

Echidnapping! Call the cops!

Knock-knock.

Who's there?

Ed.

Ed who?

Edvanced medicine for pain!

Knock-knock.

Who's there?

Eddie.

Eddie who?

Eddie body home?

Knock-knock.

Who's there?

Edie.

Edie who?

Edie my hat!

Knock-knock.

Who's there?

Edith.

Edith who?

Edithd me on the lipth!

Knock-knock.

Who's there?

Effie.

Effie who?

Effie'd known you were coming
he'd have stayed at home!

Knock-knock.

Who's there?

Egbert.

Egbert who?

Egbert no bacon, please!

Knock-knock.

Who's there?

Egg.

Egg who?

Egg-cited to meet you!

Knock-knock.

Who's there?

Egg.

Egg who?

Egg-sactly!

Knock-knock.

Who's there?

Egg.

Egg who?

Egg-stremely cold waiting for you
to open the door!

Knock-knock.

Who's there?

Egypt.

Egypt who?

Egypt a bit off my best china plate!

Knock-knock.

Who's there?

Egypt.

Egypt who?

Egypt me out in the cold!

Knock-knock.

Who's there?

Egypt.

Egypt who?

Egypt you when he sold you a broken doorbell!

Knock-knock.

Who's there?

Eight.

Eight who?

Eight me out of house and home!

THE A-Z OF KNOCK-KNOCK JOKES

Knock-knock.
Who's there?
Eileen.
Eileen who?
Eileen Don your bell and broke it!

Knock-knock.
Who's there?
Eisenhower.
Eisenhower who?
Eisenhower late for school this morning!

Knock-knock.
Who's there?
Elaine.
Elaine who?
Elaine of the freeway!

Knock-knock.

Who's there?

Elektra.

Elektra who?

Elektra circuit – shocking!

Knock-knock.

Who's there?

Element.

Element who?

Element to tell you that she
can't see you today!

Knock-knock.

Who's there?

Elephant.

Elephant who?

Elephant-a-sizes about being a Hollywood star!

Knock-knock.
Who's there?
Eli.
Eli who?
Eli, Eli O!

Knock-knock.
Who's there?
Eli.
Eli who?
Elis all the time!

Knock-knock.
Who's there?
Eliza.
Eliza who?
Eliza wake at night thinking about this door!

Knock-knock.

Who's there?

Elizabeth.

Elizabeth who?

Elizabeth of knowledge is a dangerous thing!

Knock-knock.

Who's there?

Elke.

Elke who?

Elke Seltzer – plop, plop, fizz!

Knock-knock.

Who's there?

Ella.

Ella who?

Ella-vator. Doesn't that give you a lift?

Knock-knock.

Who's there?

Ella man.

Ella man who?

Ella man-tary, my dear Watson!

Knock-knock.

Who's there?

Ellen.

Ellen who?

I've been through Ellen high water to get here!

Knock-knock.

Who's there?

Ellen.

Ellen who?

Ellen-eed is love!

Knock-knock.
Who's there?
Ellie.
Ellie who?
Ellie-phants never forget!

Knock-knock.
Who's there?
Miss Ellie.
Miss Ellie who?
Miss Ellie good films recently?

Knock-knock.
Who's there?
Ellis.
Ellis who?
Ellis before 'M'!

Knock-knock.

Who's there?

Ellis.

Ellis who?

Ellis damnation!

Knock-knock.

Who's there?

Elsie.

Elsie who?

Elsie you later!

Knock-knock.

Who's there?

Elton.

Elton who?

Elton old lady to cross the road!

Knock-knock.
Who's there?
Elvis.
Elvis who?
Elvis-eeing you around soon!

Knock-knock.
Who's there?
Emile.
Emile who?
Emile fit for a king!

Knock-knock.
Who's there?
Emma.
Emma who?
Emma pig when it comes to ice cream!

Knock-knock.

Who's there?

Emmett.

Emmett who?

Emmett the back door, not the front!

Knock-knock.

Who's there?

Emu.

Emu who?

Emu are a lovely couple!

Knock-knock.

Who's there?

Enid.

Enid who?

Enid spanking for being so rude!

Knock-knock.

Who's there?

Enoch.

Enoch who?

Enoch and Enoch but no one answers the door!

Knock-knock.

Who's there?

Erica.

Erica who?

Erica'd the last sweet!

Knock-knock.

Who's there?

Erin.

Erin who?

Erin your tyres makes your bike go better!

Knock-knock.

Who's there?

Erna.

Erna who?

Erna living!

Knock-knock.

Who's there?

Ernie.

Ernie who?

Ernie plenty of money, are you?

Knock-knock.

Who's there?

Eskimo.

Eskimo who?

Eskimo questions, I'll tell you no lies!

Knock-knock.

Who's there?

Esme.

Esme who?

Esme petticoat hanging down at the back?

Knock-knock.

Who's there?

Esther.

Esther who?

Esther anything I can do for you?

Knock-knock.

Who's there?

Ethan.

Ethan who?

Ethan people don't go to church!

Knock-knock.

Who's there?

Ethan.

Ethan who?

Ethan me out of house and home you are!

Knock-knock.

Who's there?

Etta.

Etta who?

Etta-quette!

Knock-knock.

Who's there?

Eucalyptus.

Eucalyptus who?

Eucalyptus on that bill –
we want our money back!

Knock-Knock.
Who's there?
Ether.
Ether who?
Ether Bunny!
Knock-Knock.
Who's there?
Nother.
Nother who?
Nother Ether Bunny!
Knock-Knock.
Who's there?
Stella.
Stella who?
Stella nother Ether Bunny!
Knock Knock.
Who's there?
Beep-beep.
Beep-beep who?
Car go beep-beep run all over the Ether Bunnies!
Knock knock.
Who's there?
Boo.
Boo who?
Don't cry, there'll be nother Ether Bunny
next Ether!

Knock-knock.

Who's there?

Eugenie.

Eugenie who?

Eugenie, me Tarzan!

Knock-knock.

Who's there?

Eugenie.

Eugenie who?

Eugenie from the bottle who will grant me three wishes?

Knock-knock.

Who's there?

Eumenides.

Eumenides who?

Eumenides trousers and I won't tell that you ripped them!

Knock-knock.

Who's there?

Eunice.

Eunice who?

Eunice boy, let me in!

Knock-knock.

Who's there?

Euripides.

Euripides who?

Euripides trousers and you'll
pay for a new pair!

Knock-knock.

Who's there?

Europe.

Europe who?

Europe-ning the door too slow, hurry up!

THE A-Z OF KNOCK-KNOCK JOKES

Knock-knock.
Who's there?
Europe.
Europe who?
Europe early this morning!

Knock-knock.
Who's there?
Eustace.
Eustace who?
Come Eustace you are!

Knock-knock.
Who's there?
Eva.
Eva who?
Eva you're deaf or your doorbell isn't working!

Knock-knock.

Who's there?

Evadne.

Evadne who?

Evadne problems with your teeth?

Knock-knock.

Who's there?

Evan.

Evan who?

Evan you should know who it is!

Knock-knock.

Who's there?

Evan.

Evan who?

Evan and Earth!

Knock-knock.

Who's there?

Eve.

Eve who?

Eve-ho my hearties!

Knock-knock.

Who's there?

Evi.

Evi who?

Evi thing's coming up roses!

Knock-knock.

Who's there?

Ewan.

Ewan who?

No, just me!

Knock-knock.

Who's there?

Eye.

Eye who?

Eye know who you are!

Knock-knock.

Who's there?

Eyes.

Eyes who?

Eyes got loads more knock-knock jokes for you!

Knock-knock.

Who's there?

Eyesore.

Eyesore who?

Eyesore do like you!

Knock-knock.

Who's there?

Ezra.

Ezra who?

Ezra room to rent?

FG

Knock-knock

Who's there?

Ferdie.

Ferdie who ?

Ferdie last time open this door!

Knock-knock.

Who's there?

Francis.

Francis who?

Francis full of French people!

Knock-knock

Who's there?

Fred.

Fred who ?

Fred I've got some bad news.

THE A-Z OF KNOCK-KNOCK JOKES

Knock-knock.
Who's there?
Freeze.
Freeze who?
Freeze a jolly good fellow!

Knock-knock.
Who's there?
Georgia.
Georgia who?
Georgia the Jungle – watch out for that tree!

Knock-knock.
Who's there?
Ghost.
Ghost who?
Ghost-art the show, the crowd's waiting!

Knock-knock
Who's there?
Gladys.
Gladys who ?
Gladys my last joke, I'll bet.

Knock-knock.
Who's there?
Goanna.
Goanna who?
Goanna open the door!

Knock-knock
Who's there?
Gus.
Gus who?
That's what you're supposed to do!

Knock-knock
Who's there?
Hacienda.
Hacienda who?
Hacienda the story.

Knock-knock.
Who's there?
Hank.
Hank who?
You're welcome!

Knock-knock.
Who's there?
Harry.
Harry who?
Harry up and open the door!

Knock-knock.

Who's there?

Hatch.

Hatch who?

Bless you and please cover your mouth next time!

Knock-knock

Who's there?

Heaven.

Heaven who?

Heaven seen you in ages!

Knock-knock

Who's there?

Heifer.

Heifer who ?

Heifer heard so many bad jokes?

Knock-knock.
Who's there?
Henna.
Henna who?
Henna-thing you want!

Knock-knock.
Who's there?
Hewlett.
Hewlett who?
Hewlett all of these mosquitoes in?

Knock-knock.
Who's there?
Hide-out.
Hide-out who?
Hide-out you can stop being annoying!

Knock-knock.

Who's there?

Holden.

Holden who?

Holden the other end of the rope!

Knock-knock.

Who's there?

Honey bee.

Honey bee who?

Honey, bee a sweetie and get me a cup of tea!

Knock-knock.

Who's there?

House.

House who?

House it going, dude?

Knock-knock
Who's there?
Howard.
Howard who?
Howard I know?

Knock-knock.
Who's there?
Huron.
Huron who?
Huron time for once!

Knock-knock.

Who's there?

I don't know.

I don't know who?

I told you I don't know.

Why don't you believe me?

If you didn't see me for one day

would you remember me?

Yes!

If you didn't see me for one week

would you remember me?

Yes!

If you didn't see me for one month

would you still remember me?

Yes!

Knock-knock.

Who's there?

Hey, you told me you would remember me!

Knock-knock.

Who's there?

I love.

I love who?

How am I supposed to know? You tell me!

Knock-knock.

Who's there?

Ian.

Ian who?

Ian a lot of money!

Knock-knock.

Who's there?

Ice-cream.

Ice-cream who?

Ice-cream if you don't let me in!

Knock-knock.

Who's there?

Ice-cream.

Ice-cream who?

Ice-cream of Jeannie!

Knock-knock.

Who's there?

Ichabod.

Ichabod who?

Ichabod night out, can I borrow an umbrella?

Knock-knock.

Who's there?

Icy.

Icy who?

I see you're wearing no underwear!

Knock-knock.

Who's there?

Ida.

Ida who?

Ida-umped all my problems in your lap!

Knock-knock.

Who's there?

Ida.

Ida who?

Ida know why I love you like I do!

Knock-knock.

Who's there?

Ida.

Ida who?

Idaho, not Ida-who! Can't you say it right?

Knock-knock.

Who's there?

Ida.

Ida who?

Ida face, she's so ugly!

Knock-knock.

Who's there?

Ida.

Ida who?

Ida terrible time getting here!

Knock-knock.

Who's there?

Idaho.

Idaho who?

Idahoed the whole garden but I was tired!

Knock-knock.
Who's there?
Igloo.
Igloo who?
Igloo knew Suzie like I know Suzie . . .

Knock-knock.
Who's there?
Iguana.
Iguana who?
Iguana hold your hand!

Knock-knock.
Who's there?
Ike.
Ike who?
Ike-n't stop laughing!

Knock-knock.
Who's there?
Illegal.
Illegal who?
Illegal stays in the nest until it feels better!

Knock-knock.
Who's there?
Ilka.
Ilka who?
Ilka-pone!

Knock-knock.
Who's there?
Ilona.
Ilona who?
Ilona Ranger!

Knock-knock.

Who's there?

Ima.

Ima who?

Ima girl who can't say no!

Knock-knock.

Who's there?

Imogen.

Imogen who?

Imogen life without chocolate!

Knock-knock.

Who's there?

Ina.

Ina who?

Ina minute I'm going to knock this door down!

Knock-knock.

Who's there?

Ina Claire.

Ina Claire who?

Ina Claire day, you can see forever!

Knock-knock.

Who's there?

India.

India who?

India night time I go to sleep!

Knock-knock.

Who's there?

Indiana.

Indiana who?

Indianals of history you'll be famous!

Knock-knock.

Who's there?

Indonesia.

Indonesia who?

I look at you and get weak Indonesia!

Knock-knock.

Who's there?

Ines.

Ines who?

Ines-pecial place to hide your presents!

Knock-knock.

Who's there?

Ingrid.

Ingrid who?

Ingrid sorrow I have to leave you!

Knock-knock.

Who's there?

Insect.

Insect who?

Insect your name here!

Knock-knock.

Who's there?

Iona.

Iona who?

Iona a great train set!

Knock-knock.

Who's there?

Iowa.

Iowa who?

Iowa you a dollar!

THE A-Z OF KNOCK-KNOCK JOKES

Knock-knock.

Who's there?

Ira.

Ira who?

Ira-te, or soon will be if you don't let me in!

Knock-knock.

Who's there?

Iran.

Iran who?

Iran away when you answered before!

Knock-knock.

Who's there?

Iraq.

Iraq who?

Iraq of lamb!

Knock-knock.

Who's there?

Ireland.

Ireland who?

Ireland you some money if you promise to pay me back!

Knock-knock.

Who's there?

Irene.

Irene who?

Irene and Irene but still no one answers the door!

Knock-knock.

Who's there?

Iris.

Iris who?

Iris Tew in the name of the law!

Knock-knock.

Who's there?

Iris.

Iris who?

Iris you were here!

Knock-knock.

Who's there?

Irish.

Irish who?

Irish you would come out and play with me!

Knock-knock.

Who's there?

Irma.

Irma who?

Irma big girl now!

Knock-knock.

Who's there?

Isaac.

Isaac who?

Isaacly who do you think this is?

Knock-knock.

Who's there?

Isabel.

Isabel who?

Isabel broken? I had to knock!

Knock-knock.

Who's there?

Isadore.

Isadore who?

Isadore locked? I can't get in!

Knock-knock.
Who's there?
Isaiah.
Isaiah who?
Isaiah again, knock-knock!

Knock-knock.
Who's there?
Isla.
Isla who?
Isla be seeing you!

Knock-knock.
Who's there?
Island.
Island who?
Island on your roof with my parachute!

Knock-knock.

Who's there?

Istvan.

Istvan who?

Istvan to be alone!

Knock-knock.

Who's there?

Ivan.

Ivan who?

Ivan my money back now!

Knock-knock.

Who's there?

Ivan.

Ivan who?

Ivan idea you don't want to see me!

Knock-knock.

Who's there?

Ivan.

Ivan who?

Ivan-vested all my money in the stock market!

Knock-knock.

Who's there?

Ivana.

Ivana who?

Ivana be rich!

Knock-knock.

Who's there?

Ivanhoe.

Ivanhoe who?

Ivan, hoe the crop please!

Knock-knock.

Who's there?

Ivor.

Ivor who?

Ivor sore hand from knocking on your door!

Knock-knock.

Who's there?

Ivory.

Ivory who?

Ivory strong like Tarzan!

Knock-knock.

Who's there?

Ivy.

Ivy who?

Ivy got you under my skin!

THE A-Z OF KNOCK-KNOCK JOKES

Knock-knock.
Who's there?
Izzy.
Izzy who?
Izzy at the door? You'd better answer it then!

Knock-knock.
Who's there?
Izzy.
Izzy who?
Izzy come, Izzy go!

Knock-knock.
Who's there?
Izzy.
Izzy who?
Izzy Moe than you can handle?

Knock-knock.

Who's there?

Jack.

Jack who?

Jack Potts!

Knock-knock.

Who's there?

Jackie.

Jackie who?

Jackien that job, it doesn't pay enough!

Knock-knock.

Who's there?

Jackson.

Jackson who?

Jackson the telephone, you'd better answer it!

Knock-knock.

Who's there?

Jacqueline.

Jacqueline who?

Jacqueline and Hyde!

Knock-knock.

Who's there?

Jacques.

Jacques who?

Jacques of all trades!

Knock-knock.

Who's there?

Jade.

Jade who?

Jade a whole cake today!

Knock-knock.
Who's there?
Jagger.
Jagger who?
Jaggerd edge!

Knock-knock.
Who's there?
Jaguar.
Jaguar who?
Jaguar nimble, Jaguar quick!

Knock-knock.
Who's there?
Jam.
Jam who?
Jam-ind, I'm trying to get out!

THE A-Z OF KNOCK-KNOCK JOKES

Knock-knock.

Who's there?

Jamaica.

Jamaica who?

Jamaica mistake?

Knock-knock.

Who's there?

James.

James who?

James people play . . .

Knock-knock.

Who's there?

Jamie.

Jamie who?

Jamie a game of chess!

Knock-knock.

Who's there?

Jamie.

Jamie who?

Jamien you don't recognise my voice?

Knock-knock.

Who's there?

Jan.

Jan who?

Jan of Green Gables!

Knock-knock.

Who's there?

Janet.

Janet who?

Janet has too many holes in it,
the fish will escape!

Knock-knock.

Who's there?

Jano.

Jano who?

Janotice how easy it is to get past Security?

Knock-knock.

Who's there?

Japan.

Japan who?

Japan is too hot, ouch!

Knock-knock.

Who's there?

Jasmine.

Jasmine who?

Jasmine like to play in quartets!

Knock-knock.

Who's there?

Jason.

Jason who?

Jason a rainbow!

Knock-knock.

Who's there?

Java.

Java who?

Java dog in your house?

Knock-knock.

Who's there?

Jaws.

Jaws who?

Jaws truly!

THE A-Z OF KNOCK-KNOCK JOKES

Knock-knock.

Who's there?

Jay.

Jay who?

Jaylbird with clanking chains!

Knock-knock.

Who's there?

Jean.

Jean who?

Jean-ius, you just don't recognise it!

Knock-knock.

Who's there?

Jeff.

Jeff who?

Jeff in one ear, shout!

Knock-knock.

Who's there?

Jefferson.

Jefferson who?

Jefferson yourself on a sun deck?

Knock-knock.

Who's there?

Jeffrey.

Jeffrey who?

Jeffrey time you ask me who I am!

Knock-knock.

Who's there?

Jenny.

Jenny who?

Jennyd any help opening the door?

Knock-knock.
Who's there?
Jenny.
Jenny who?
Jenny-men prefer blondes!

Knock-knock.
Who's there?
Jenny Lind.
Jenny Lind who?
Jenny, Lind me some money!

Knock-knock.
Who's there?
Jeritza.
Jeritza who?
Jeritza your limit an hour ago!

Knock-knock.

Who's there?

Jerome.

Jerome who?

Jerome where you want to!

Knock-knock.

Who's there?

Jerrold.

Jerrold who?

Jerrold friend, that's who!

Knock-knock.

Who's there?

Jerry.

Jerry who?

Jerryusalem, Jerryusalem . . .

Knock-knock.
Who's there?
Jess.
Jess who?
Jess me and my shadow!

Knock-knock.
Who's there?
Jess.
Jess who?
I give up, who?

Knock-knock.
Who's there?
Jess.
Jess who?
Jess one of those things!

Knock-knock.

Who's there?

Jesse.

Jess who?

Jesse-bell!

Knock-knock.

Who's there?

Jesse.

Jesse who?

Jesse if you can recognise my voice!

Knock-knock.

Who's there?

Jessica.

Jessica who?

Jessica more than I thought!

Knock-knock.

Who's there?

Jester.

Jester who?

Jester minute, I'm trying to find my keys!

Knock-knock.

Who's there?

Jethro.

Jethro who?

Jethro the boat and stop talking so much!

Knock-knock.

Who's there?

Jewell.

Jewell who?

Jewell remember me when you see my face!

Knock-knock.

Who's there?

Jez.

Jez who?

Jez a minute!

Knock-knock.

Who's there?

Jilly.

Jilly who?

Jilly out here, so let me in!

Knock-knock.

Who's there?

Jim.

Jim who?

Jim mind if we come in?

Knock-knock.

Who's there?

Jimmy.

Jimmy who?

Jimmy a little kiss on the cheek!

Knock-knock.

Who's there?

Jo.

Jo who?

Jo jump in a lake!

Knock-knock.

Who's there?

Jo.

Jo who?

Jokes are fun, especially knock-knocks!

Knock-knock.

Who's there?

Joan.

Joan who?

Joan you remember me?

Knock-knock.

Who's there?

Joanna.

Joanna who?

Joanna big kiss?

Knock-knock.

Who's there?

Joanne.

Joanne who?

Joanne tell!

Knock-knock.

Who's there?

Joe.

Joe who?

Joe away, I'm not talking to you!

Knock-knock.

Who's there?

Joe Namath!

Joe Namath who?

Joe Namath not on the door,
that's why I knocked!

Knock-knock.

Who's there?

Joe-jum.

Joe-jum who?

Joe-jum-poff a cliff!

Knock-knock.

Who's there?

Joey.

Joey who?

Joey to the centre of the Earth!

Knock-knock.

Who's there?

Johannes.

Johannes who?

Johannes are cold!

Knock-knock.

Who's there?

John.

John who?

John with the Wind!

Knock-knock.

Who's there?

John.

John who?

John me in a cup of tea?

Knock-knock.

Who's there?

Joplin.

Joplin who?

Joplin any time you like!

Knock-knock.

Who's there?

Jose.

Jose who?

Jose you can see!

Knock-knock.

Who's there?

Josette.

Josette who?

Josette down and be quiet!

Knock-knock.

Who's there?

Joyce.

Joyce who?

Joyce of a new generation!

Knock-knock.

Who's there?

Juan.

Juan who?

Juan to hear some more of these?

Knock-knock.

Who's there?

Juan.

Juan who?

Juan of these days you'll find out!

Knock-knock.

Who's there?

Juan.

Juan who?

Juandering star!

Knock-knock.

Who's there?

Juana.

Juana who?

Juana go out with me?

Knock-knock.

Who's there?

Juanita.

Juanita who?

Juanita nother burger?

Knock-knock.

Who's there?

Judd.

Judd who?

Juddgement Day!

Knock-knock.

Who's there?

Jude.

Jude who?

Jude doubt me? Just open the door!

Knock-knock.
Who's there?
Judy.
Judy who?
Judy liver milk still?

Knock-knock.
Who's there?
Juice.
Juice who?
Juice still want to know?

Knock-knock.
Who's there?
Juicy.
Juicy who?
Juicy that rude sign on the door?

Knock-knock.
Who's there?
Julia.
Julia who?
Julia want to come in!

Knock-knock.
Who's there?
Julian.
Julian who?
Julian I are going out now!

Knock-knock.
Who's there?
Julie.
Julie who?
Julie-vous couchez avec moi?

Knock-knock.
Who's there?
Julie.
Julie who?
Julie your door unlocked?

Knock-knock.
Who's there?
Juliet.
Juliet who?
Juliet the same amount but she's OK . . .

Knock-knock.
Who's there?
Juliet.
Juliet who?
Juliet me in or not?

Knock-knock.

Who's there?

July.

July who?

July to me about stealing my pencil?

Knock-knock.

Who's there?

June.

June who?

June know how to open this door?

Knock-knock.

Who's there?

June.

June who?

Juneed to be so annoying?

THE A-Z OF KNOCK-KNOCK JOKES

Knock-knock.
Who's there?
Juno.
Juno who?
I dunno, Juno?

Knock-knock.
Who's there?
Jupiter.
Jupiter who?
Jupiter hurry, or you'll miss the bus!

Knock-knock.
Who's there?
Jupiter.
Jupiter who?
Jupiter fly in my soup?

Knock-knock.

Who's there?

Jussi.

Jussi who?

Jussi fruit!

Knock-knock.

Who's there?

Justice!

Justice who?

Justice I thought, no one home!

Knock-knock.

Who's there?

Justice.

Justice who?

Justice once won't you be quiet?

Knock-knock.

Who's there?

Justin.

Justin who?

Justin Casey howls, give him his bottle!

Knock-knock.

Who's there?

Justin.

Justin who?

Justin Quire who is at the door . . .

K

Knock-knock.
Who's there?
K-2.
K-2 who?
K-2 come in!

Knock-knock.
Who's there?
Kanga.
Kanga who?
Kangarry come out to play?

Knock-knock.
Who's there?
Kanga.
Kanga who?
No, kangaroo!

Knock-knock.

Who's there?

Kareem.

Kareem who?

Kareem of the crop!

Knock-knock.

Who's there?

Karen.

Karen who?

Karen the can for you!

Knock-knock.

Who's there?

Kathy.

Kathy who?

Kathy-ou again?

Knock-knock.

Who's there?

Katie.

Katie who?

Katie Lang!

Knock-knock.

Who's there?

Kay.

Kay who?

Kay, L ,M, N ,O, P, Q, R, S, T, U, V, W, X, Y, Z!

Knock-knock.

Who's there?

Kay.

Kay who?

Kay sera sera!

Knock-knock.

Who's there?

Keanu.

Keanu who?

Keanu let me in? It's cold out here!

Knock-knock.

Who's there?

Keith.

Keith who?

Keith your hands off me!

Knock-knock.

Who's there?

Keith.

Keith who?

Keith me, thweetheart!

Knock-knock.

Who's there?

Ken.

Ken who?

Ken you open the door and let me in?

Knock-knock.

Who's there?

Kendall.

Kendall who?

Kendall and Barbie go together!

Knock-knock.

Who's there?

Kenneth.

Kenneth who?

Kenneth little kids play with you!

Knock-knock.
Who's there?
Kent.
Kent who?
Kent you tell who it is?

Knock-knock.
Who's there?
Kentucky.
Kentucky who?
Kentucky too well, have a sore throat!

Knock-knock.
Who's there?
Kenya.
Kenya who?
Kenya guess who it is?

Knock-knock.

Who's there?

Kermit.

Kermit who?

Kermit a crime and you'll get locked up!

Knock-knock.

Who's there?

Kerry.

Kerry who?

Kerry me on your shoulders, Dad!

Knock-knock.

Who's there?

Ketchup.

Ketchup who?

Ketchup with me and I'll tell you!

Knock-knock.

Who's there?

Ketchup.

Ketchup who?

Ketchup the tree again!

Knock-knock.

Who's there?

Khan.

Khan who?

Khan to where the flavour is!

Knock-knock.

Who's there?

Khomeini.

Khomeini who?

Khomeini old time for dinner!

Knock-knock.

Who's there?

Kiki.

Kiki who?

Kiki's stuck in the lock, let me in!

Knock-knock.

Who's there?

Kim.

Kim who?

Kim too late!

Knock-knock.

Who's there?

King Kong.

King Kong who?

King Kong's now part of China!

Knock-knock.

Who's there?

Kipper.

Kipper who?

Kipper hands to yourself!

Knock-knock.

Who's there?

Kit.

Kit who?

Kit me quick!

Knock-knock.

Who's there?

Kitty.

Kitty who?

Kittyzen Kane!

Knock-knock.
Who's there?
Kiwi.
Kiwi who?
Kiwi-t any longer!

Knock-knock.
Who's there?
Klaus.
Klaus who?
Klaus as two sticks!

Knock-knock.
Who's there?
Knee.
Knee who?
Knee-d you ask?

Knock-knock.
Who's there?
Knees.
Knees who?
Knees you every day!

Knock-knock.
Who's there?
Koch.
Koch who?
Koch in the act!

Knock-knock.
Who's there?
Kojak.
Kojak who?
Kojak up the car, I've got a flat tyre!

THE A-Z OF KNOCK-KNOCK JOKES

Knock-knock.
Who's there?
Kookaburra.
Kookaburra who?
Kookaburramundi for dinner!

Knock-knock.
Who's there?
Kristin.
Kristin who?
Kristin the baby in church!

Knock-knock.
Who's there?
Kurt.
Kurt who?
Kurt and wounded!

Knock-knock.

Who's there?

Kurt and Conan.

Kurt and Conan who?

Kurt and Conan down on the last act!

Knock-knock.

Who's there?

Kyle.

Kyle who?

Kyle be good if you let me in!

Knock-knock.

Who's there?

Kyoto.

Kyoto who?

Kyoto jail, do not pass go, do not collect $200!

Knock-knock.
Who's there?
Lacy.
Lacy who?
Lacy as the day is long!

Knock-knock.
Who's there?
Lady.
Lady who?
Lady law down!

Knock-knock.
Who's there?
Lana.
Lana who?
Lana the free!

Knock-knock.

Who's there?

Laos.

Laos who?

Laos and found!

Knock-knock.

Who's there?

Larry.

Larry who?

Larry Krishna!

Knock-knock.

Who's there?

Larva.

Larva who?

Larva cup of coffee!

Knock-knock.
Who's there?
Laser.
Laser who?
Laser faire!

Knock-knock.
Who's there?
Lass.
Lass who?
That's what cowboys use, isn't it?

Knock-knock.
Who's there?
Lass.
Lass who?
Lass time I saw Paris!

THE A-Z OF KNOCK-KNOCK JOKES

Knock-knock.
Who's there?
Latin.
Latin who?
Latin me in would be a good idea!

Knock-knock.
Who's there?
Lauren.
Lauren who?
Lauren order!

Knock-knock.
Who's there?
Laurie.
Laurie who?
Laurie-load of goodies!

Knock-knock.

Who's there?

Leaf.

Leaf who?

Leaf me alone!

Knock-knock.

Who's there?

Leah.

Leah who?

Leah-n an egg for my breakfast!

Knock-knock.

Who's there?

Lech.

Lech who?

Lech in the lurch!

Knock-knock.

Who's there?

Lee.

Lee who?

Lee me alone! I've got a headache!

Knock-knock.

Who's there?

Lee.

Lee who?

Leed on Macduff!

Knock-knock.

Who's there?

Lee King.

Lee King who?

Lee King bucket!

Knock-knock.

Who's there?

Leland.

Leland who?

Leland of the free and the home of the brave!

Knock-knock.

Who's there?

Lemming.

Lemming who?

Lemming tree very pretty,
and the lemon flower is sweet!

Knock-knock.

Who's there?

Lemon.

Lemon who?

Lemon me give you a kiss!

Knock-knock.

Who's there?

Len.

Len who?

Len us a fiver, will you?

Knock-knock.

Who's there?

Lena.

Lena who?

Lena little closer and I'll tell you!

Knock-knock.

Who's there?

Lenin.

Lenin who?

Lenin tree has good fruit!

Knock-knock.
Who's there?
Lenny.
Lenny who?
Lenny in, I'm hungry!

Knock-knock.
Who's there?
Leon.
Leon who?
Leonly one for me!

Knock-knock.
Who's there?
Leonie.
Leonie who?
Leonie one I love!

Knock-knock.

Who's there?

Les.

Les who?

Les go out for a picnic!

Knock-knock.

Who's there?

Les.

Les who?

Les high and dry!

Knock-knock.

Who's there?

Leslie.

Leslie who?

Leslie town now before they catch us!

Knock-knock.

Who's there?

Lester.

Lester who?

Lestern over a new leaf!

Knock-knock.

Who's there?

Letter.

Letter who?

Letter in!

Knock-knock.

Who's there?

Lettuce.

Lettuce who?

Lettuce try again tomorrow!

Knock-knock.
Who's there?
Letty.
Letty who?
Letty it all hang out!

Knock-knock.
Who's there?
Lewis.
Lewis who?
Lewis all my money gambling!

Knock-knock.
Who's there?
Lieder.
Lieder who?
Lieder of the pack!

Knock-knock.
Who's there?
Lief.
Lief who?
Lief me alone!

Knock-knock.
Who's there?
Lilac.
Lilac who?
Lilac a trooper!

Knock-knock.
Who's there?
Lillian.
Lillian who?
Lillian the garden!

THE A-Z OF KNOCK-KNOCK JOKES

Knock-knock.

Who's there?

Lily.

Lily who?

Lily House on the Prairie!

Knock-knock.

Who's there?

Lima Bean.

Lima Bean who?

Lima Bean working on the railroad . . .

Knock-knock.

Who's there?

Linda.

Linda who?

Linda hand, I can't be expected to do it
all by myself!

Knock-knock.

Who's there?

Lion.

Lion who?

Lion on your doorstep, open up!

Knock-knock.

Who's there?

Lionel.

Lionel who?

Lionel roar if you don't feed him!

Knock-knock.

Who's there?

Lionel.

Lionel who?

Lionel get you nowhere, better tell the truth!

Knock-knock.

Who's there?

Lisa.

Lisa who?

Lisa new car from only $199 a month!

Knock-knock.

Who's there?

Lisa.

Lisa who?

Lisa you can do is let me in!

Knock-knock.

Who's there?

Lisbon.

Lisbon who?

Lisbon married eight times!

Knock-knock.
Who's there?
Listz.
Listz who?
Listz of ingredients!

Knock-knock.
Who's there?
Little old lady.
Little old lady who?
Didn't know you could yodel!

Knock-knock.
Who's there?
Livia.
Livia who?
Livia me alone!

Knock-knock.

Who's there?

Liz.

Liz who?

Liz-en to me when I'm talking to you!

Knock-knock.

Who's there?

Liza.

Liza who?

Liza wrong to tell!

Knock-knock.

Who's there?

Lizard.

Lizard who?

Lizard like to stay Queen for another ten years!

Knock-knock.

Who's there?

Llama.

Llama who?

Llama Yankee Doodle Dandy . . .

Knock-knock.

Who's there?

Lloyd.

Lloyd who?

He Lloyd to me, he said it was Wednesday
and it's only Tuesday!

Knock-knock.

Who's there?

Lloyd.

Lloyd who?

Lloyd a horse to water but you can't make it drink!

Knock-knock.

Who's there?

Lock.

Lock who?

Lock who it is after all this time!

Knock-knock.

Who's there?

Lodz.

Lodz who?

Lodz of fun!

Knock-knock.

Who's there?

Lolly.

Lolly who?

Lolly-ing about on the floor!

Knock-knock.
Who's there?
Lon.
Lon who?
Lon in the tooth!

Knock-knock.
Who's there?
Lotte.
Lotte who?
Lotte sense!

Knock-knock.
Who's there?
Lou.
Lou who?
Lous your money at the races?

Knock-knock.
Who's there?
Louis.
Louis who?
Louis-n up!

Knock-knock.
Who's there?
Louise.
Louise who?
Louise coming to tea today!

Knock-knock.
Who's there?
Louisiana.
Louisiana who?
Louisiana boyfriend split up!

Knock-knock.

Who's there?

Luc.

Luc who?

Luc for the silver lining!

Knock-knock.

Who's there?

Lucerne.

Lucerne who?

Lucerne some maths today!

Knock-knock.

Who's there?

Lucetta.

Lucetta who?

Lucetta tricky problem!

Knock-knock.

Who's there?

Lucifer.

Lucifer who?

Lucifer coat and you'll be cold!

Knock-knock.

Who's there?

Lucille.

Lucille who?

Lucille-ings are dangerous if you are tall!

Knock-knock.

Who's there?

Lucinda.

Lucinda who?

Lucinda chain, I want to get in!

Knock-knock.
Who's there?
Lucinda.
Lucinda who?
Lucinda sky with diamonds!

Knock-knock.
Who's there?
Lucretia.
Lucretia who?
Lucretia from the Black Lagoon!

Knock-knock.
Who's there?
Lucy.
Lucy who?
Lucy Lastic can be embarrassing!

Knock-knock.
Who's there?
Luigi.
Luigi who?
Luigi board!

Knock-knock.
Who's there?
Luke.
Luke who?
Luke through the keyhole and see!

Knock-knock.
Who's there?
Lulu.
Lulu who?
Lulu's not working, can I use yours?

Knock-knock.
Who's there?
Lydia.
Lydia who?
Lydia teapot is cracked!

Knock-knock.
Who's there?
Lyle.
Lyle who?
Lyle low till the police have gone!

Knock-knock.
Who's there?
Lyndon.
Lyndon who?
Lyndon ear and I'll tell you!

M

Knock-knock.

Who's there?

Madam.

Madam who?

Madam foot is caught in your door!

Knock-knock.

Who's there?

Mafia.

Mafia who?

Mafia killing me.

Knock-knock.

Who's there?

Mary.

Mary who?

Mary me and I'll be your sweetheart forever!

Knock-knock.

Who's there?

Mary-lee.

Mary-lee who?

Mary-lee we roll along, roll along, roll along . . .

Knock-knock.

Who's there?

Matthew.

Matthew who?

Matthew lace came undone, can you tie it?

Knock-knock.

Who's there?

Mice.

Mice who?

Mice to meet you!

Knock-knock.

Who's there?

Mikey.

Mikey who?

Mikey doesn't fit in the keyhole!

Knock-knock.

Who's there?

Miniature.

Miniature who?

Miniature open the door, I'll tell you!

Knock-knock.

Who's there?

Minneapolis.

Minneapolis who?

Minneapolis a day keeps the doctor away!

Knock-knock.
Who's there?
Minnie.
Minnie who?
Minnie more!

Knock-knock.
Who's there?
Minsk.
Minsk who?
Minsk meat!

Knock-knock.
Who's there?
Minviz.
Minviz who?
'minvizible. Help!

Knock-knock.
Who's there?
Monkey.
Monkey who?
Monkey see, Monkey do!

Knock-knock.
Who's there?
Moo.
Moo who?
Please make your mind up –
are you a cow or an owl?

Knock-knock.
Who's there?
Moose.
Moose who?
Moose you be so nosy?

Knock-knock.

Who's there?

Moscow.

Moscow who?

Moscow gives more milk than pa's cow!

Knock-knock.

Who's there?

Mother.

Mother who?

Mother-in-law here for the weekend!

Knock-knock.

Who's there?

Murray cod.

Murray cod who?

Murray cod a code. Got a hankie?

N

Knock-knock.
Who's there?
N-8.
N-8 who?
N-8 tendencies!

Knock-knock.
Who's there?
Nan.
Nan who?
Nanswer me or I'll go away!

Knock-knock.
Who's there?
Nana.
Nana who?
Nana, hey, hey, kiss him goodbye!

THE A-Z OF KNOCK-KNOCK JOKES

Knock-knock.
Who's there?
Nana.
Nana who?
Nana your business!

Knock-knock.
Who's there?
Nancy.
Nancy who?
Nancy a biscuit?

Knock-knock.
Who's there?
Nanny.
Nanny who?
Nanny one at home?

Knock-knock.

Who's there?

Nantucket.

Nantucket who?

Nantucket, but she'll have to give it back!

Knock-knock.

Who's there?

Nate.

Nate who?

Nate-ure boy!

Knock-knock.

Who's there?

N-E.

N-E who?

N-E body you like, so long as you let me in!

Knock-knock.
Who's there?
Neal.
Neal who?
Neal and pray!

Knock-knock.
Who's there?
Nebraska.
Nebraska who?
Nebraska girl for a date, she might say ycs!

Knock-knock.
Who's there?
Ned.
Ned who?
Ned and neck!

Knock-knock.
Who's there?
Nell.
Nell who?
Nell is hot!

Knock-knock.
Who's there?
Nero.
Nero who?
Nero far!

Knock-knock.
Who's there?
Nettie.
Nettie who?
Nettie as a fruitcake!

THE A-Z OF KNOCK-KNOCK JOKES

Knock-knock.

Who's there?

Nevada.

Nevada who?

Nevada saw you look so bad –
you should be in bed!

Knock-knock.

Who's there?

Nicholas.

Nicholas who?

Nicholas girls shouldn't climb trees!

Knock-knock.

Who's there?

Nick.

Nick who?

Nick-nack paddy-wack, give the dog a bone . . .

Knock-knock.
Who's there?
Nine.
Nine who?
Nine danke!

Knock-knock.
Who's there?
No one.
No one who?
I said NO ONE!

Knock-knock.
Who's there?
Noah.
Noah who?
Noah good place to eat?

Knock-knock.

Who's there?

Noah.

Noah who?

Noah yes – which is it?

Knock-knock.

Who's there?

Noah.

Noah who?

Noah-body knows the trouble I've seen . . .

Knock-knock.

Who's there?

Noah.

Noah who?

Noah good place to find more jokes?

Knock-knock.
Who's there?
Nobel.
Nobel who?
Nobel so I'll knock!

Knock-knock.
Who's there?
Nobody.
Nobody who?
Just nobody!

Knock-knock.
Who's there?
Noel.
Noel who?
Noel E. Phant is going to poke
his trunk into my business!

Knock-knock.

Who's there?

Noise.

Noise who?

Noise to see you!

Knock-knock.

Who's there?

Nola.

Nola who?

Nola-ner driver may drive a car alone!

Knock-knock.

Who's there?

Nome.

Nome who?

Nome-an is an island!

Knock-knock.

Who's there?

Norma Lee.

Norma Lee who?

Norma Lee I ring the doorbell,
but you don't have one!

Knock-knock.

Who's there?

Norman.

Norman who?

Norman's land!

Knock-knock.

Who's there?

Norton.

Norton who?

Norton cocaine is stupid!

Knock-knock.

Who's there?

Norway.

Norway who?

Norway will I leave till you open the door!

Knock-knock.

Who's there?

Nose.

Nose who?

I nose plenty more knock-knock jokes,
don't worry!

Knock-knock.

Who's there?

Nougat.

Nougat who?

Nougat can go that fast!

Knock-knock.

Who's there?

Nuisance.

Nuisance who?

What's nuisance yesterday?

Knock-knock.

Who's there?

Nunya.

Nunya who?

Nunya business, buddy!

Knock-knock.

Who's there?

Nurse.

Nurse who?

Nurse sense talking to you!

Knock-knock.
Who's there?
Oasis.
Oasis who?
Oasis, let your sister in!

Knock-knock.
Who's there?
Oboe.
Oboe who?
Oboe, I've got the wrong address!

Knock-knock.
Who's there?
Ocelot.
Ocelot who?
Ocelot of questions, don't you?

Knock-knock.

Who's there?

Odel-lay-he.

Odel-lay-he who?

Didn't know you could yodel!

Knock-knock.

Who's there?

Odessa.

Odessa who?

Odessa really funny face, man!

Knock-knock.

Who's there?

Odette.

Odette who?

Odette's a bad sign!

Knock-knock.

Who's there?

Odysseus.

Odysseus who?

Odysseus the last straw!

Knock-knock.

Who's there?

Offenbach.

Offenbach who?

Offenbach is performed!

Knock-knock.

Who's there?

Ogre.

Ogre who?

Ogre take a flying leap!

Knock-knock.
Who's there?
Ogre.
Ogre who?
Ogre the hill!

Knock-knock.
Who's there?
Oil.
Oil who?
Oil be seeing you then!

Knock-knock.
Who's there?
Oily.
Oily who?
Oily bird catches the worm!

Knock-knock.

Who's there?

Okra.

Okra who?

Okra Winfrey!

Knock-knock.

Who's there?

O. J.

O. J. who?

You were on the jury!

Knock-knock.

Who's there?

Olaf.

Olaf who?

Olaf if you think it's that funny!

Knock-knock.

Who's there?

Old King Cole.

Old King Cole who?

Old King Cole, so turn the heat up!

Knock-knock.

Who's there?

Oldest son.

Oldest son who?

Oldest son shines bright on
my old Kentucky home . . .

Knock-knock.

Who's there?

Ole!

Ole who?

Ole little town of Bethlehem . . .

Knock-knock.

Who's there?

Olga.

Olga who?

Olga home if you don't open up!

Knock-knock.

Who's there?

Olive.

Olive who?

Olive none of your lip!

Knock-knock.

Who's there?

Olive.

Olive who?

Olive just around the corner!

Knock-knock.
Who's there?
Olive.
Olive who?
Olive you!

Knock-knock.
Who's there?
Oliver.
Oliver who?
Oliver, but she doesn't love me!

Knock-knock.
Who's there?
Oliver.
Oliver who?
Oliver troubles are over!

Knock-knock.
Who's there?
Olivia.
Olivia who?
Olivia me alone!

Knock-knock.
Who's there?
Olivia.
Olivia who?
Olivia but I lost the key!

Knock-knock.
Who's there?
Oman.
Oman who?
Oman, you are cute!

Knock-knock.

Who's there?

Omar.

Omar who?

Omar goodness, I got the wrong address!

Knock-knock.

Who's there?

Omega.

Omega who?

Omega best man win!

Knock-knock.

Who's there?

Omelette.

Omelette who?

Omelette-in you kiss me!

Knock-knock.

Who's there?

Omelette.

Omelette who?

Omelette smarter than you think!

Knock-knock.

Who's there?

One.

One who?

One-der why you keep asking that?

Knock-knock.

Who's there?

One.

One who?

One't you come home, Bill Bailey,
won't you come home . . .

Knock-knock.

Who's there?

One-Eye.

One-Eye who?

You're the One-Eye care for!

Knock-knock.

Who's there?

Onya.

Onya who?

Onya marks, get set, go!

Knock-knock.

Who's there?

Ooze.

Ooze who?

Ooze been sleeping in my bed?

Knock-knock.

Who's there?

Opera.

Opera who?

Opera-tunity, and you thought
opportunity only knocked once!

Knock-knock.

Who's there?

Orange.

Orange who?

Orange you even going to open the door?

Knock-knock.

Who's there?

Orange juice.

Orange juice who?

Orange juice sorry you asked?

Knock-knock.

Who's there?

Orest.

Orest who?

Orest that man!

Knock-knock.

Who's there?

Organ.

Organ who?

Organ-ise a party, it's my birthday!

Knock-knock.

Who's there?

Orson.

Orson who?

Orson cart!

Knock-knock.

Who's there?

Osborn.

Osborn who?

Osborn today, it's my birthday!

Knock-knock.

Who's there?

Oscar.

Oscar who?

Oscar a silly question, get a silly answer!

Knock-knock.

Who's there?

O'Shea.

O'Shea who?

O'Shea that's a sad story!

Knock-knock.

Who's there?

Oslo.

Oslo who?

Oslo down, what's the hurry?

Knock-knock.

Who's there?

Oswald.

Oswald who?

Oswald my chewing gum!

Knock-knock.

Who's there?

Oswego.

Oswego who?

Oswego marching, marching home . . .

Knock-knock.
Who's there?
Othello.
Othello who?
Othello you thalked to me!

Knock-knock.
Who's there?
Otis.
Otis who?
Otis a wonderful day for a walk in the park!

Knock-knock.
Who's there?
Ottawa.
Ottawa who?
Ottawa know you're telling the truth?

THE A-Z OF KNOCK-KNOCK JOKES

Knock-knock.
Who's there?
Oui.
Oui who?
Oui will, oui will rock you!

Knock-knock.
Who's there?
Owen.
Owen who?
Owen are you going to let me in?

Knock-knock.
Who's there?
Owl.
Owl who?
Owl I can say is 'knock-knock'!

THE A-Z OF KNOCK-KNOCK JOKES

Knock-knock.

Who's there?

Owl.

Owl who?

Owl be sad if you don't let me in!

Knock-knock.

Who's there?

Owl.

Owl who?

Owl you know unless you open the door?

Knock-knock.

Who's there?

Oz.

Oz who?

Oz got something for you!

Knock-knock.
Who's there?
Ozzie.
Ozzie who?
Ozzie you later!

Knock-knock.

Who's there?

P

P who?

P-nuts are an elephant's favourite treat!

Knock-knock.

Who's there?

Pablo.

Pablo who?

Pablo your horn!

Knock-knock.

Who's there?

Packer.

Packer who?

Packer morons!

Knock-knock.
Who's there?
Paine.
Paine who?
Paine in the neck!

Knock-knock.
Who's there?
Pam.
Pam who?
Pam-per yourself!

Knock-knock.
Who's there?
Pammy.
Pammy who?
Pammy the key, the door is locked!

Knock-knock.

Who's there?

Panon.

Panon who?

Panon my intrusion!

Knock-knock.

Who's there?

Panther.

Panther who?

Panther what you wear on your legth!

Knock-knock.

Who's there?

Paris.

Paris who?

Paris the thought!

Knock-knock.
Who's there?
Paris.
Paris who?
Paris the salt, please!

Knock-knock.
Who's there?
Parsley.
Parsley who?
Parsley the sauce, please!

Knock-knock.
Who's there?
Parton.
Parton who?
Parton my French!

267

Knock-knock.
Who's there?
Passion.
Passion who?
Passion through and I thought I'd say hello!

Knock-knock.
Who's there?
Pasta.
Pasta who?
Pasta pepper, please!

Knock-knock.
Who's there?
Pastille.
Pastille who?
Pastille long road you'll find a village!

Knock-knock.

Who's there?

Pasture.

Pasture who?

Pasture bedtime isn't it?

Knock-knock.

Who's there?

Pat.

Pat who?

Pat up your troubles in your old kit bag . . .

Knock-knock.

Who's there?

Pat.

Pat who?

Pat a loose end!

Knock-knock.

Who's there?

Pat.

Pat who?

Pat yourself on the back!

Knock-knock.

Who's there?

Patrick.

Patrick who?

Patricked me into coming!

Knock-knock.

Who's there?

Patsy.

Patsy who?

Patsy dog on the head, he likes it!

Knock-knock.

Who's there?

Patty.

Patty who?

Patty cake, patty cake, baker's man . . .

Knock-knock.

Who's there?

Paul.

Paul who?

Paul a fast one!

Knock-knock.

Who's there?

Paul.

Paul who?

Paul aboard!

Knock-knock.
Who's there?
Paul and Portia.
Paul and Portia who?
Paul and Portia door to open it!

Knock-knock.
Who's there?
Paulie.
Paulie who?
Paulie fast one!

Knock-knock.
Who's there?
Pear.
Pear who?
Pear of shoes!

Knock-knock.

Who's there?

Pears.

Pears who?

Pears the party?

Knock-knock.

Who's there?

Peas.

Peas who?

Peas got the whole world in his hands . . .

Knock-knock.

Who's there?

Peas.

Peas who?

Peas to meet you!

Knock-knock.

Who's there?

Pecan.

Pecan who?

Pecan work it out!

Knock-knock.

Who's there?

Pecan.

Pecan who?

Pecan someone your own size!

Knock-knock.

Who's there?

Peg.

Peg who?

Peg your pardon, I've got the wrong door!

Knock-knock.

Who's there?

Pen.

Pen who?

Pent up emotions!

Knock-knock.

Who's there?

Pencil.

Pencil who?

Your pencil fall down if the elastic breaks!

Knock-knock.

Who's there?

Penny.

Penny who?

Penny for your thoughts!

Knock-knock.

Who's there?

Penny.

Penny who?

Penny-sylvania Station!

Knock-knock.

Who's there?

Pepsi.

Pepsi who?

Pepsi through the keyhole!

Knock-knock.

Who's there?

Percy.

Percy who?

Percy Vere and you'll succeed!

Knock-knock.

Who's there?

Perry.

Perry who?

Perry well, thank you!

Knock-knock.

Who's there?

Perth.

Perth who?

Perth full of money!

Knock-knock.

Who's there?

Peru.

Peru who?

Peru your point!

Knock-knock.
Who's there?
Petal.
Petal who?
Petal fast, it's a steep hill!

Knock-knock.
Who's there?
Peter.
Peter who?
Peter bread and butter!

Knock-knock.
Who's there?
Pharaoh.
Pharaoh who?
Pharaoh-nough!

Knock-knock.

Who's there?

Phil.

Phil who?

Phil up my hot-water bottle, I'm cold!

Knock-knock.

Who's there?

Phil.

Phil who?

Philthy lucre!

Knock-knock.

Who's there?

Philip.

Philip who?

Philip the tank, I've got a long way to go!

Knock-knock.

Who's there?

Phineas.

Phineas who?

Phineas thing happened on the way
to the forum!

Knock-knock.

Who's there?

Phoebe.

Phoebe who?

Phoebe too high for us to pay!

Knock-knock.

Who's there?

Phone.

Phone who?

Phone I'd known it was you!

Knock-knock.
Who's there?
Phyllis.
Phyllis who?
Phyllis in on the news!

Knock-knock.
Who's there?
Piaf.
Piaf who?
Piaf your bills!

Knock-knock.
Who's there?
Piano.
Piano who?
Piano Ferries!

Knock-knock.

Who's there?

Pickle.

Pickle who?

Oh, that's my favourite wind instrument!

Knock-knock.

Who's there?

Pierre.

Pierre who?

Pierre through the keyhole and you'll see!

Knock-knock.

Who's there?

Pikachu.

Pickachu who?

I'll pikachu, then you peek at me!

Knock-knock.

Who's there?

Pill.

Pill who?

Yes please, and a sheet to go with it!

Knock-knock.

Who's there?

Ping-pong.

Ping-pong who?

Ping-pong the witch is dead . . .

Knock-knock.

Who's there?

Pinza.

Pinza who?

Pinza needles!

Knock-knock.
Who's there?
Pits.
Pits who?
Pits my party and I'll cry if I want to!

Knock-knock.
Who's there?
Pizza.
Pizza who?
Pizza cake would be great right now!

Knock-knock.
Who's there?
Plato.
Plato who?
Plato fish and chips, please!

THE A-Z OF KNOCK-KNOCK JOKES

Knock-knock.
Who's there?
Plums.
Plums who?
Plums me that we'll always be friends!

Knock-knock.
Who's there?
Poker.
Poker who?
Poker and see if she's awake!

Knock-knock.
Who's there?
Police.
Police who?
Police open the door!

Knock-knock.

Who's there?

Polly.

Polly who?

Polly the other one, it's got bells on it!

Knock-knock.

Who's there?

Pollyanna.

Pollyanna who?

Pollyanna bad kid when you get to know her!

Knock-knock.

Who's there?

Pop.

Pop who?

Pop over to the shop for me!

Knock-knock.

Who's there?

Poppy.

Poppy who?

Poppy-n any time you like!

Knock-knock.

Who's there?

Portia.

Portia who?

Portia the door, it's stuck!

Knock-knock.

Who's there?

Posa.

Posa who?

Posa question!

Knock-knock.

Who's there?

Prussia.

Prussia who?

Prussia cooker!

Knock-knock.

Who's there?

Pudding.

Pudding who?

Pudding on your shoes before your trousers
is a bad idea!

Knock-knock.

Who's there?

Pulp.

Pulp who?

Pulp hard on the door, it's stiff!

Knock-knock.

Who's there?

Puss.

Puss who?

Puss your bike, it's safer!

Knock-knock.

Who's there?

Pyjamas.

Pyjamas who?

Pyjamas around me and hold me tight!

Knock-knock.

Who's there?

Python.

Python who?

Python with your pocket money!

R

Knock-knock.

Who's there?

Razor.

Razor who?

Razor hands up, buddy, this is a stick up!

Knock-knock.

Who's there?

Repeat.

Repeat who?

Who, who, who!

Knock-knock.

Who's there?

Rudolph.

Rudolph the red-nosed reindeer?

No, money is the Rudolph all evil!

Knock-knock.

Who's there?

Russell.

Russell Crowe?

No, Russell up some grub!

S

Knock-knock.

Who's there?

Sadie.

Sadie who?

Sadie magic words and I'll tell you!

Knock-knock.

Who's there?

Sarah.

Sarah who?

Sarah doctor in the house?

Knock-knock.

Who's there?

Shari.

Shari who?

Shari your lunch with me, and I'll share
mine with you!

Knock-knock.

Who's there?

Shark.

Shark who?

Shark a leg!

Knock-knock.

Who's there?

Sheila.

Sheila who?

Sheila-oves to play piano!

Knock-knock.

Who's there?

Shelby.

Shelby who?

Shelby comin' round the mountain
when she comes . . .

Knock-knock.
Who's there?
Snow.
Snow who?
Snow business like show business . . .

Knock-knock.
Who's there?
Spank.
Spank who?
Spank you!

Knock-knock.
Who's there?
Statue.
Statue who?
Statue or someone else?

Knock-knock.

Who's there?

Stew.

Stew who?

Stew early to go to bed!

Knock-knock.
Who's there?
Tad.
Tad who?
Tad's all folks!

Knock-knock.
Who's there?
Taipei.
Taipei who?
Taipei sixty words a minute is pretty fast!

Knock-knock.
Who's there?
Talbot.
Talbot who?
Talbot too thin!

THE A-Z OF KNOCK-KNOCK JOKES

Knock-knock.
Who's there?
Tamara.
Tamara who?
Tamara is Tuesday, today is Monday!

Knock-knock.
Who's there?
Tamara.
Tamara who?
Tamara the world!

Knock-knock.
Who's there?
Tamsin.
Tamsin who?
Tamsin time again I came to the wrong house!

Knock-knock.

Who's there?

Tango!

Tango who?

Tango faster than this if you want!

Knock-knock.

Who's there?

Tania!

Tania who?

Tania self around, you'll see!

Knock-knock.

Who's there?

Tank.

Tank who?

You're welcome!

THE A-Z OF KNOCK-KNOCK JOKES

Knock-knock.
Who's there?
Tara.
Tara who?
Tara-ra boom-de-ay!

Knock-knock.
Who's there?
Tarzan.
Tarzan who?
Tarzan stripes forever . . .

Knock-knock.
Who's there?
Tariq.
Tariq who?
Tariq of perfume will put anyone off!

Knock-knock.

Who's there?

Teacher.

Teacher who?

Teacher to go knocking on my door
in the middle of the night!

Knock-knock.

Who's there?

Teddy.

Teddy who?

Teddy is the beginning of the rest of your life!

Knock-knock.

Who's there?

Teheran.

Teheran who?

Teheran and look me in the eye!

THE A-Z OF KNOCK-KNOCK JOKES

Knock-knock.

Who's there?

Telly.

Telly who?

Telly your friend to come out!

Knock-knock.

Who's there?

Ten.

Ten who?

Ten to your own business!

Knock-knock.

Who's there?

Tennessee.

Tennessee who?

Tennessee you tonight?

Knock-knock.

Who's there?

Tennessee.

Tennessee who?

Tennessee is played at Wimbledon!

Knock-knock.

Who's there?

Tennis.

Tennis who?

Tennis five plus five!

Knock-knock.

Who's there?

Teresa.

Teresa who?

Teresa Green!

THE A-Z OF KNOCK-KNOCK JOKES

Knock-knock.
Who's there?
Termite.
Termite who?
Termite's the night!

Knock-knock.
Who's there?
Terry.
Terry who?
Terry's nothing like a dame . . .

Knock-knock.
Who's there?
Tex.
Tex who?
Tex two to tango!

Knock-knock.

Who's there?

Texas.

Texas who?

Texas are getting higher every year!

Knock-knock.

Who's there?

Thad.

Thad who?

Thad's the way, uh-huh, uh-huh, I like it . . .

Knock-knock.

Who's there?

Thaddeus.

Thaddeus who?

To be or not to be, Thaddeus the question . . .

Knock-knock.

Who's there?

Thatcher.

Thatcher who?

Thatcher could get away with it!

Knock-knock.

Who's there?

Thayer.

Thayer who?

Thayer thorry and I won't throw thish pie in your face!

Knock-knock.

Who's there?

Thea.

Thea who?

Thea later, alligator!

Knock-knock.

Who's there?

Thelma.

Thelma who?

Thelma your soul!

Knock-knock.

Who's there?

Thelonius.

Thelonius who?

Thelonius kid in town!

Knock-knock.

Who's there?

Theodore.

Theodore who?

Theodore wasn't open so I knock-knocked!

Knock-knock.

Who's there?

Theresa.

Theresa who?

Theresa fly in my soup!

Knock-knock.

Who's there?

Thermos.

Thermos who?

Thermos be a better knock-knock joke than this!

Knock-knock.

Who's there?

Theron.

Theron who?

Theronheit or Centigrade? I always get mixed up!

Knock-knock.

Who's there?

Thighs.

Thighs who?

Thighs the limit!

Knock-knock.

Who's there?

Thistle.

Thistle who?

Thistle be the last time I knock on this door!

Knock-knock.

Who's there?

Thistle.

Thistle who?

Thistle have to keep you going until the
dinner's ready . . .

Knock-knock.
Who's there?
Three.
Three who?
Three surgeon!

Knock-knock.
Who's there?
Throat.
Throat who?
Throat to me!

Knock-knock.
Who's there?
Throne.
Throne who?
Throne out the baby with the bathwater!

Knock-knock.

Who's there?

Thrush.

Thrush who?

Thrushow must go on!

Knock-knock.

Who's there?

Thumb.

Thumb who?

Thumb like it hot and thumb like it cold!

Knock-knock.

Who's there?

Thumping.

Thumping who?

Thumping green and slimy is
climbing up your back!

Knock-knock.

Who's there?

Thurston.

Thurston who?

Thurston' and hungerin'!

Knock-knock.

Who's there?

Tibet.

Tibet who?

Early Tibet and early to rise . . .

Knock-knock.

Who's there?

Tic-tac.

Tic-tac who?

Tic-tac paddy-whack, give the dog a bone . . .

Knock-knock.

Who's there?

Tick.

Tick who?

Tick 'em up and give me all your money!

Knock-knock.

Who's there?

Tiffany.

Tiffany who?

Tiffany rubbish out the bin, will you?

Knock-knock.

Who's there?

Tillie.

Tillie who?

Tillie comes I'm going to wait here!

Knock-knock.

Who's there?

Tilly.

Tilly who?

Tilly-vision is my favourite invention!

Knock-knock.

Who's there?

Tim.

Tim who?

Tim after time . . .

Knock-knock.

Who's there?

Tina.

Tina who?

Tina salmon!

Knock-knock.

Who's there?

Tinker Bell.

Tinker Bell who?

Tinker Bell is out of order!

Knock-knock.

Who's there?

Tish.

Tish who?

That's good for wiping your nose!

Knock-knock.

Who's there?

Tito.

Tito who?

Titotaller!

Knock-knock.

Who's there?

Titus.

Titus who?

Titus it can be!

Knock-knock.

Who's there?

Toast.

Toast who?

Toast where the days!

Knock-knock.

Who's there?

Tobias.

Tobias who?

Tobias a pig, that's why I went to market!

Knock-knock.

Who's there?

Toby.

Toby who?

Toby or not Toby, that is the question . . .

Knock-knock.

Who's there?

Tom Sawyer.

Tom Sawyer who?

Tom Sawyer underwear!

Knock-knock.

Who's there?

Tommy.

Tommy who?

Tommy you will always be gorgeous!

Knock-knock.
Who's there?
Too whit.
Too whit who?
Is there an owl in the place?

Knock-knock.
Who's there?
Toodle.
Toodle who?
Bye, bye!

Knock-knock.
Who's there?
Toot.
Toot who?
Toot the bitter end!

Knock-knock.

Who's there?

Tooth.

Tooth who?

Tooth or dare!

Knock-knock.

Who's there?

Toothy.

Toothy who?

Toothy the day after Monday!

Knock-knock.

Who's there?

Topic.

Topic who?

Topic a wildflower isn't allowed!

Knock-knock.

Who's there?

Torch.

Torch who?

Torch you'd never ask!

Knock-knock.

Who's there?

Tori.

Tori who?

Tori I bumped into you!

Knock-knock.

Who's there?

Toronto.

Toronto who?

Toronto be a law against knock-knock jokes!

Knock-knock.

Who's there?

Toto.

Toto who?

Toto-lly devoted to you!

Knock-knock.

Who's there?

Toucan.

Toucan who?

Toucan live as cheaply as one!

Knock-knock.

Who's there?

Toyota.

Toyota who?

Toyota be a law against such awful jokes!

Knock-knock.

Who's there?

Trey.

Trey who?

Trey of the Lonesome Pine!

Knock-knock.

Who's there?

Tricia.

Tricia who?

Bless you!

Knock-knock.

Who's there?

Tristan.

Tristan who?

Tristan Isolde than his brother!

Knock-knock.

Who's there?

Trixie.

Trixie who?

Trixie couldn't do because he was a bad magician!

Knock-knock.

Who's there?

Troy.

Troy who?

Troy the bell instead!

Knock-knock.

Who's there?

Trudy.

Trudy who?

Trudy your word!

Knock-knock.

Who's there?

Truffle.

Truffle who?

Truffle with you is that you are so shy!

Knock-knock.

Who's there?

Truman.

Truman who?

Truman and good needed for the jury!

Knock-knock.

Who's there?

Trump.

Trump who?

Trumped up charges!

Knock-knock.

Who's there?

Tuba.

Tuba who?

Tuba toothpaste!

Knock-knock.

Who's there?

Tubby.

Tubby who?

Tubby or not to be . . .

Knock-knock.

Who's there?

Tucson.

Tucson who?

Tucson and two daughters are enough kids!

Knock-knock.

Who's there?

Tummy.

Tummy who?

Tummy you'll always be No. 1!

Knock-knock.

Who's there?

Tuna.

Tuna who?

You can tuna piano, but you can't tuna fish!

Knock-knock.

Who's there?

Tuna.

Tuna who?

Tuna your radio down, I'm trying to get some sleep!

Knock-knock.
Who's there?
Tunis.
Tunis who?
Tunis company, three's a crowd!

Knock-knock.
Who's there?
Turin.
Turin who?
Turin a deaf ear!

Knock-knock.
Who's there?
Turkey.
Turkey who?
Turkey, open door!

Knock-knock.

Who's there?

Turner.

Turner who?

Turner round, what is that behind you?

Knock-knock.

Who's there?

Turnip.

Turnip who?

Turnip for work at nine or you're fired!

Knock-knock.

Who's there?

Twain.

Twain who?

Twain station!

Knock-knock.
Who's there?
Twig.
Twig who?
Twig or tweat?

Knock-knock.
Who's there?
Twyla.
Twyla who?
Twyla-ight of the gods!

Knock-knock.
Who's there?
Ty.
Ty who?
Ty breaker!

Knock-knock.
Who's there?
Typhoid.
Typhoid who?
Typhoid that song before!

Knock-knock.
Who's there?
Tyrone.
Tyrone who?
Tyrone shoelaces!

Knock-knock.
Who's there?
Tyson.
Tyson who?
Tyson of this on for size!

Knock-knock.
Who's there?
U-4.
U-4 who?
U-4 me and me for you . . .

Knock-knock.
Who's there?
U-8.
U-8 who?
U-8 my lunch!

Knock-knock.
Who's there?
U-boat!
U-boat who?
U-boat can play with me today!

Knock-knock.

Who's there?

UB-40.

UB-40 who?

UB-40 today – happy birthday!

Ring-Ring.

Who's there?

UCI.

UCI who?

UCI had to ring because you didn't answer when I knocked!

Knock-knock.

Who's there?

Uganda.

Uganda who?

Uganda get away with this!

Knock-knock.
Who's there?
Uluru.
Uluru who?
Uluru the day!

Knock-knock.
Who's there?
Una.
Una who?
No I don't, tell me!

Knock-knock.
Who's there?
Unite.
Unite who?
Unite a person, you call him Sir!

Knock-knock.
Who's there?
Urchin.
Urchin who?
Urchin is pointed!

Knock-knock.
Who's there?
Uriah.
Uriah who?
Keep Uriah on the ball!

Knock-knock.
Who's there?
Uruguay.
Uruguay who?
You go Uruguay and I'll go mine!

Knock-knock.
Who's there?
Usher.
Usher who?
Usher wish you would let me in!

Knock-knock.
Who's there?
Utah.
Utah who?
Utah sight, utah mind!

Knock-knock.
Who's there?
Utica.
Utica who?
Utica high road and I'll take the low road . . .

Knock-knock.
Who's there?
Uva.
Uva who?
Uva vacuum!

VW

Knock-knock.

Who's there?

Venue.

Venue who?

Venue gonna open this door?

Knock-knock.

Who's there?

Wah.

Wah who?

Hey man, no need to get so excited about it!

Knock-knock.

Who's there?

Wanda.

Wanda who?

Wanda buy some Girl Scout cookies?

Knock-knock.

Who's there?

Water.

Water who?

Water you answering the door for?

Knock-knock.

Who's there?

Wayne.

Wayne who?

Wayne a manger . . .

Knock-knock.

Who's there?

Wenceslas.

Wenceslas who?

Wenceslas train home?

Knock-knock.

Who's there?

Wendy.

Wendy who?

Wendy red, red robin comes bob,
bob bobbin' along . . .

Knock-knock.

Who's there?

Witchetty.

Witchetty who?

Witchetty do you want – tea or coffee?

Knock-knock.

Who's there?

Wooden shoe.

Wooden shoe who?

Wooden shoe like to know!

Knock-knock.
Who's there?
Yabbie.
Yabbie who?
Yabbie'n on holidays?

Knock-knock.
Who's there?
Yacht!
Yacht who?
Yacht-a know me by now!

Knock-knock.
Who's there?
Yachts!
Yachts who?
Yachts up, Doc?

Knock-knock.
Who's there?
Yah!
Yah who?
Ride 'em cowboy!

Knock-knock.
Who's there?
Yarra.
Yarra who?
Yarra bit of a ratbag!

Knock-knock.
Who's there?
Yehuda!
Yehuda who?
Yehuda dance all night!

Knock-knock.

Who's there?

Yellow!

Yellow who?

Yellow-ver din, can hardly hear you!

Knock-knock.

Who's there?

Yelp!

Yelp who?

Yelp me, my nose is stuck in the keyhole!

Knock-knock.

Who's there?

Yma.

Yma who?

Yma Sumad for wrecking her car!

Knock-knock.

Who's there?

Yo momma.

Yo momma who?

Seriously, it's yo momma, open the damned door!

Knock-knock.

Who's there?

Yoga!

Yoga who?

Yoga what it takes!

Knock-knock.

Who's there?

Yogi bear!

Yogi Bear who?

Yogi Bear and you'll get arrested!

Knock-knock.
Who's there?
Yolanda!
Yolanda who?
Yolanda me some money?

Knock-knock.
Who's there?
York.
York who?
York-oming over to our place!

Knock-knock.
Who's there?
You.
You who?
You who! Is there anybody in?

Knock-knock.

Who's there?

Yucatan.

Yucatan who?

Yucatan fool all people all the time . . .

Knock-knock.

Who's there?

Yuki.

Yuki who?

Yukip on saying the same boring things!

Knock-knock.

Who's there?

Yukon.

Yukon who?

Yukon go away and come back
at a reasonable time!

Knock-knock.
Who's there?
Yul.
Yul who?
Yul never guess!

Knock-knock.
Who's there?
Yuri.
Yuri who?
Yuri great friend!

Knock-knock.
Who's there?
Yvette.
Yvette who?
Yvette helps a lot of animals!

Knock-knock.

Who's there?

Yvonne.

Yvonne who?

Yvonne to be alone!

Z

Knock-knock.

Who's there?

Zaire!

Zaire who?

Zaire is polluted!

Knock-knock.

Who's there?

Zany!

Zany who?

Zany-body home?

Knock-knock.

Who's there?

Zebulon!

Zebulon who?

Zebulon to me!

Knock-knock.

Who's there?

Zeke!

Zeke who?

Zeke and you shall find!

Knock-knock.

Who's there?

Zephyr!

Zephyr who?

Zephyr de doctor, I've got a code id by node!

Knock-knock.

Who's there?

Zinka!

Zinka who?

Zinka the ship!

Knock-knock.
Who's there?
Zippy!
Zippy who?
Mrs Zippy!

Knock-knock.
Who's there?
Zippy.
Zippy who?
Zippy dee-doo-dah, zippy dee-day!

Knock-knock.
Who's there?
Zizi!
Zizi who?
Zizi when you know how!

Knock-knock.

Who's there?

Zombie!

Zombie who?

Zombies make honey, others are queens!

Knock-knock.

Who's there?

Zone!

Zone who?

Zone shadow scares him!

Knock-knock.

Who's there?

Zoo-keeper!

Zoo-keeper who?

Zoo-keeper away from me!

Knock-knock.
Who's there?
Zoom!
Zoom who?
Zoom did you expect?

Knock-knock.
Who's there?
Zsa Zsa!
Zsa Zsa who?
Zsa Zsa last knock-knock joke!

Knock-knock.
Who's there?
Zubin!
Zubin who?
Zubin eating garlic again?